WRITING DOWN THE MOON

poems & art

POEMS BY JUDYTH HILL
ART BY MARY MEADE

EVERGREEN, COLORADO

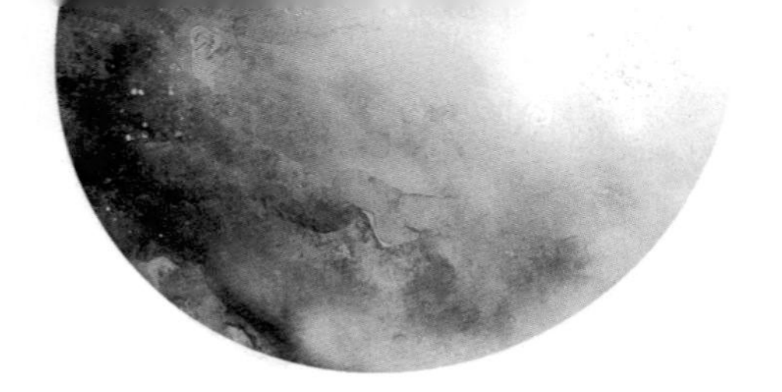

Book & Cover Design: Mary M. Meade
Circular line drawing first seen on title page: Mori Yuzan, 1919, *Han Bu Shu,* Yamda Geishu Do, Tokyo (likely)

Poems: Judyth Hill Art: Mary M. Meade

WildRisingPress.com
First Edition: ISBN 978-1-957468-13-6

CONSTANCY OF THE MOON

What is fixed, warbles.
What we stand by
holds us in its persistent light.

For Rockmirth, my Beloved,
where the Full Moon poets
gathered for many years in Her shine...
Thank you for all the joy,
all the poems,
all your Beauty.

—JH

To my family—Tenoch, Laila & Alexa.
When you are not behind me
pushing me to paint,
you are in front pulling me.

—MMM

Contents

WRITING DOWN THE MOON

Writing Down the Moon

A text for the moon would be unprintable.
Would be full one moment, empty the next.
Men become fearful, invent a religion by its irregular tick.
Women sew by its shimmer,
dresses whose folds ensnare the quick sluice of thoughts
lost down the drain, scrubbed off dishes,
swept from the hearth.

A text for the moon would be found in the children's books
my mother wrote,
on my old Smith Corona, years after her death.

Seeing it I wanted it back. Badly.
Envy for her huge body of posthumous work.
Wanting the tiny boxed set of skeleton Mariachis
pasted on her small Olivetti, with a poem,
warning *If fish is what you want,*
Fish Now.

A text for the moon would fly past, like the ribbon-feathered cranes,
overhead, perhaps thousands, going continually South,
in a dream where one plunged, afire, to earth.
I didn't know it then, how I would long to go back to those mountains
with a different love.

Quixotic text. Chocolate moon, violet moon,
rewriting itself by night,
many-petalled, many-flavoured light.
At once, shy among new greens, and dark,
a blare on the tongue seeking sweet.

A text for the Moon is recipes for cocktails, mysteriously
currant colored, sprigged with mint,
head tossed back, a shooter, gulped down.
Drunk on the letters, the double vowelling,
the soft swoony consonants.

A text for the moon would be perfumed.
Would read as hunger, and the smell,
sunwarmed hay, the last in the quiet barn.

Meaning, Maybe

Five pigeons sunning on the roof of the moon,
I mean the chapel. The one that is never open,
is maybe, a morada.

Your hand on my belly,
I mean the moon, or maybe, moonlight,
slicking my belly with tidal shadow.

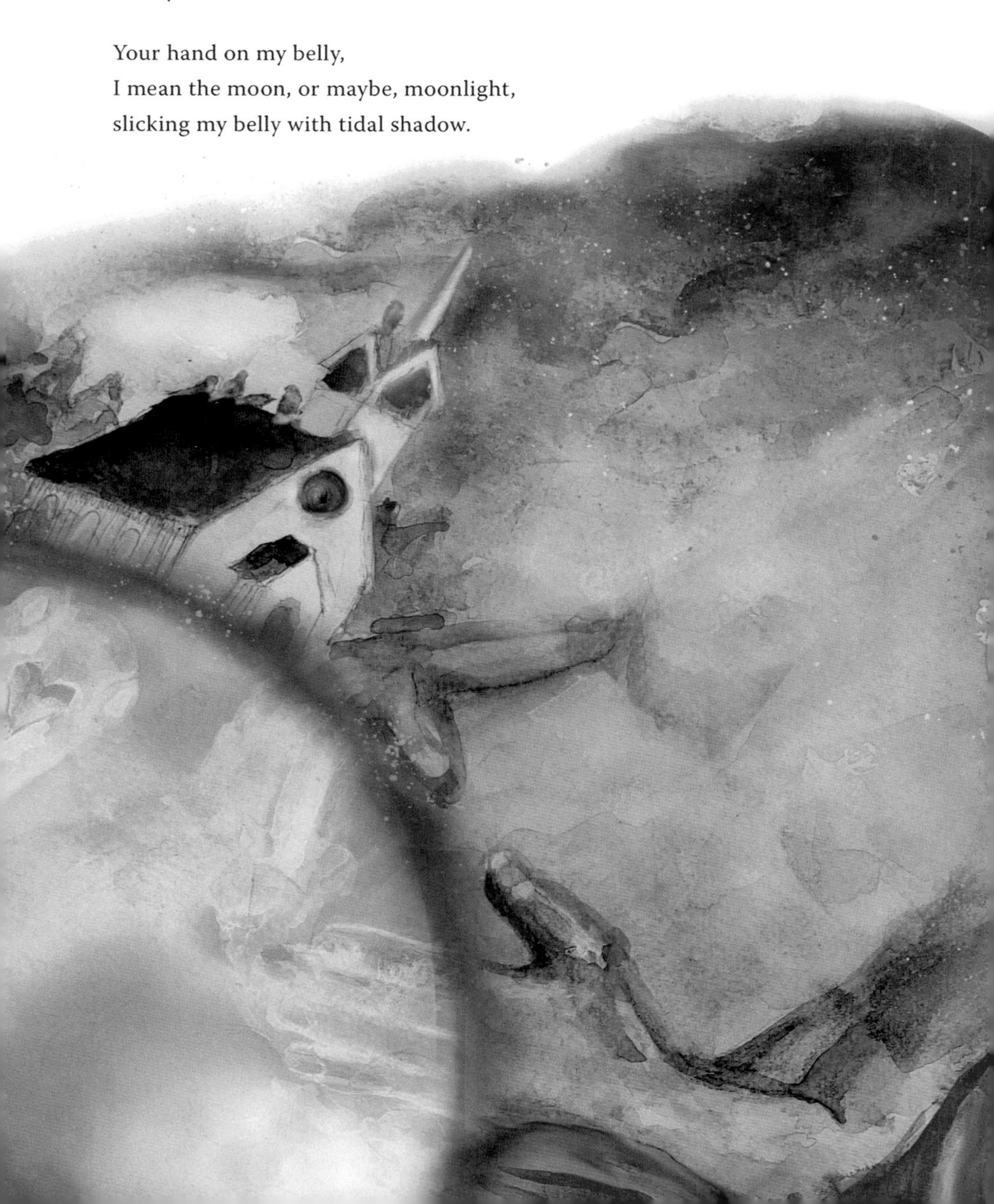

Fire in the stoves, all through the canyon.
Moonlight, I mean smoke, or maybe,
the dreams of wives, snaking silver above.

Whatever I was taught about the moon,
I mean, poetry, is wrong, maybe.
Is about honey and the hive.

Poem with No Moon

February emptied me.
I gave and got, got and gave.

Tourmaline, amber and amethyst
turned to ash and a clear plate.

I can tell the whole story now.
In the down dark, seeds wait,

rare lettuces and the moon flower:
planted every season for three summers.

And none have bloomed,
never the white, scented blossom,

promised on the seed packet,
gleaming in the dusky garden.

Cliff Notes on Moonlight

The Sprouting Grass moon writes in Esperanto
that whatever we love can go free.
Mountains skip off, unmoored,
oceans crescendo, mimicking musical epiphany,
as if they had heard Beethoven's side of the story.

Actually, also, the Sonata itself plays somewhere
in a darkened room.
Minor notes, adagio, circling a white plaster Guadalupe
lit by one votive. What else?

Prayer opens the dissonant bud,
humming bees of desire,
yearning for the outbreath of beauty.

Stung by so much wanting,
the Mare Nubium refills
a cup for the light pouring endlessly
from elsewhere.

Secret Purim Moon

Fish swimming east and light,
west and dark.
Moon on the fast track,

touch black, no backs.
Moon wearing greasepaint,
moon eating fatback.

Rosetta moon, hieroglyph of shine,
simmer in the half here,
gone again, world slung into reverse.

A hearse for the old, rehearsal for the new.

Upside down moon, the heartfelt swoon,
all of us fluent in spoken moon, tunes
drowning lunar croaking, frog lit, by night.

Hide the luminous, served on a half shell,

avec un soupçon of green cheese,
man in the
rabbit in the

No telling now, no telling.

You'll never find me,
olly oxen moon,
you be it.

Seder Moon

The Leaving Moon.
Starting over.
With less, or more?

After the Red Sea has swayed aside,
what is swept in its closing wake?

This year we don't weep. We sing.

Remember, before milk and honey,
sands stretch out for 40 years.
That's how we come by the inner waters, that other well.

After crossing, Miriam took a timbrel
in her hand, and the women went out
dancing.

She taught her people:

Half song of low winds moaning,
quarter song of stars chiming
full bass of the mountain's bellow
hollow howl in the open canyon,

Desert Moon, color of cut melon,
honeydew, shedding
a refraction of sweet, coming into glistening whole.

Moon taught her people:
how to disappear
into the new.

Shortcut to Mare Vaporum

Seems so many words are perfect, just a torrent,
and clearly, each is a seed pearl of some wisdom.
On the other side of gnosis, we can take this with a grain of salt.
All theories of Original Sin carefully spun
from fog and shadow, are set to the diurnal clock
that runs, that is perhaps pulled, by the moon.

I've heard many stories about the moon,
and told some myself, in fact, a torrent.
Every time, no matter what, there's buzz of bees, the thrum of clocks.
You could call that a kind of wisdom.
Despite whatever honey has been spun
into confectionary presence, I still taste salt.

Philosophies oxidize into salt,
then become tears falling from the seas of the moon.
Of such dark ironies are spun
the Judeo-Christian torrent
of wisdom.
Millennium? Watch Sakyamuni, laughing at the clock!

From what lit face, did we invent that clock?
From what primordial soup, did we precipitate, like salt?
Who, in their right mind, would call the answers to this, wisdom?
There's a secret kind of no thing on the moon,
a relation to original light that pours down in a torrent.
Perhaps from that certain facts were spun

and spun,
corresponding to an inner clock,
that re-imagines time as a flooding torrent
with nothing like the stable framework of salt

(whose taut latticework is also shifted by moon).
Now that's a clue to real wisdom,

in case you were seeking wisdom.
But even that can be spun
into just another theory that explains the moon
as if it were a clock,
whose hands rinse themselves in the salt
of the ocean's torrent.

Of such same salt is spun
the clock that tells not time, but wisdom
spelling a humming torrent in the frequency of moon.

Mother, May I

Lifted wings against air,
    and went out.
It was the same door as ever,
the one I hid the key to,
in your garden.
    Under cosmos,
pools of rainwater and mirrors.
    I made a spell.
I drew out
    the rules to gravitational spin
in spider web, a sticky nest
of falling.
    Then, falling,
as if I were finally that first full
moon in May, I rose
    for real.

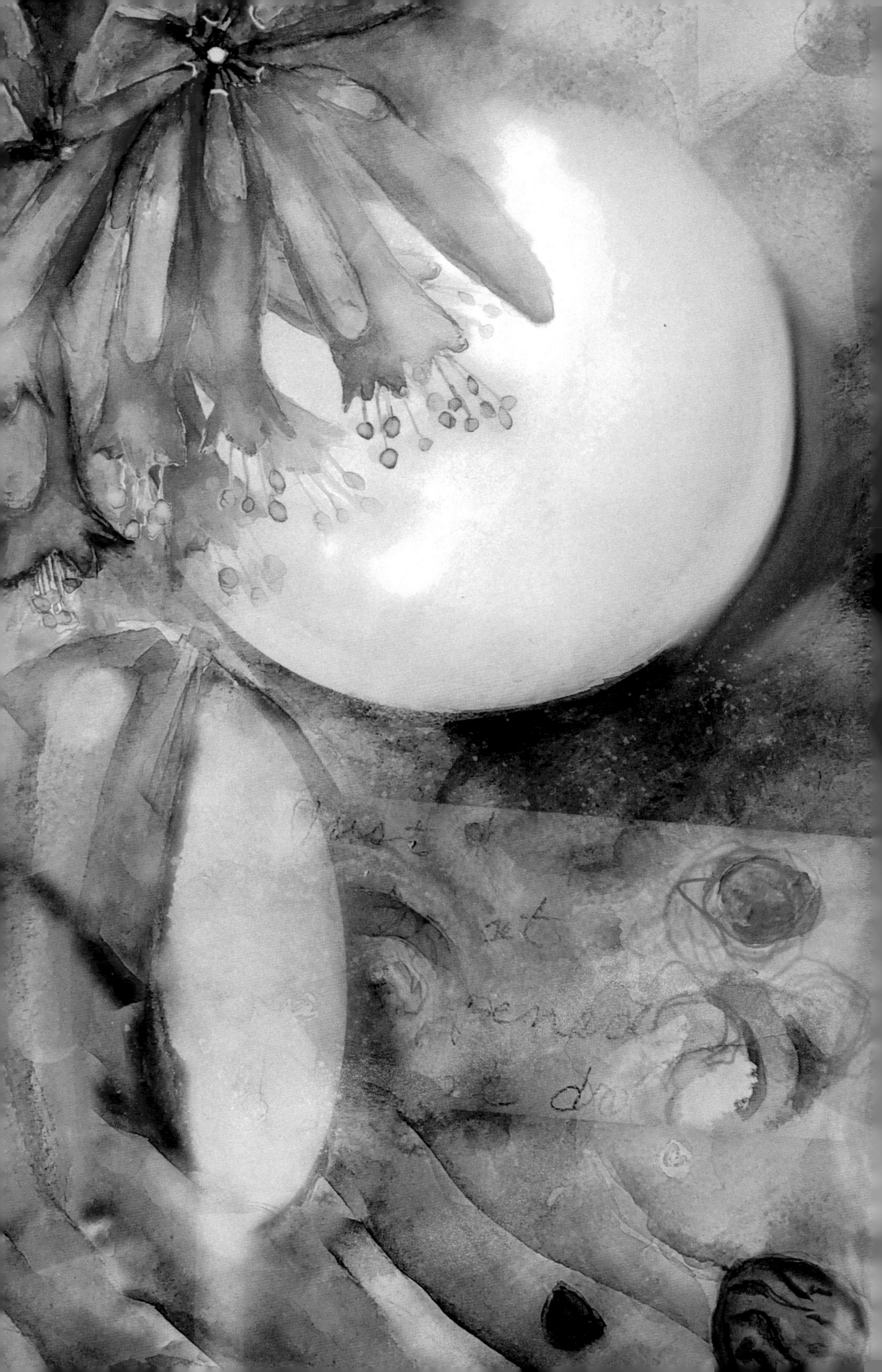

Ritual for Fires of Desire Moon

Know what is shining.
Name it.
Compose a letter to that light.
Address an envelope to the Ripe, the Seeded One, Voluptuous Olive;
    mail with a blue stamp.
Plant seeds of round fruits.
Make one white corn tortilla.
Know what comes over you so suddenly.
Write sorrow, eggplant, sacred jimson, on your left palm, and clap 3
    times.
Cover all the mirrors with green silk and honeysuckle vine.
Eat the tortilla.

A Moon Can Look at a Poet

Everyone writes about Moons.
But moons are bored of us women,
us leaky, lunar in our seasonal swing,
our wax and wane and silky pumps
that gleam moonshine on to dance floor and back again.

Click up your heels,
you slick-mooned woman,
Ride a Cock Moon to Banbury Bush.
Serve moons au gratin, moons and rice,
dip the moon lightly in wasabi and breathe fiery moon breaths.

For once, be moon. Moon all the way.
Say nothing you mean. Shift like sand.
Change daily.

Wear different bracelets every hour.
Look for silver in the cereal box,
wear your beauty in quarter phases.
Buy three silk scarves.
Talk moonwise on a street corner,
and be in just enough danger.

Be heart pounding and dry mouthed alive in a crescent way.
Shine like the sun taught you,
backwards and back at the best man in the room.

Mugs of moon juice, lunar drafts, moon on tap,
lager moon, moon wine and gibbous tea.
The moon shining in day,
is tired of reading poems about herself by women,

and would rather dress in red and go to bars
or the Goddess Café for brunch.

She'll have huevos rancheros with green chile,
too many Bloody Marys,
and ride a palomino later if she's not too drunk.
Up into the cedar hills she'll go,
if a horse could carry a moon and he can,
and the moon wants to gallop her wild self
out of women's poems anyway.

Moon Last Seen

Great horned owl, last light,
flying into the canopy of pines.

Perseid shower suspended somewhere over Sapello,
starshine tangled in my hair.

Then Green Corn Moon leaps through Jupiter, rounds the galactic
turn,
takes the sun by a nose,
straight on 'til stabled by morning, light, light and more light.

The scent of final tomatoes rhymes with autumn.

Thank you for the 68 species of aster varieties,
in late summer crescendo!

As we turn this season like a corner,
my daughter's laughter makes jam of ripened berries.

Half Way There

I have questions about the moon.
Questions about distance and what is really luminous.

That evening in the café,
how raspberries stained the white, white cloth,
and we rubbed in salt to lift the stain.
The coffee so dark, I got drunk on the essence of night.
It was bitter and delicious.

September moon rose inside me,
and also not inside me. Demi-moon
filling the room with the scent of fresh linen, shaken out,
shaken out, I opened then: stargazer lily, shed pollen and seedling,
daughter of Suzanne,
who had to die
and I had to let her.

The flavour of this moon is that whole year in reverse, a lack,
presence of absent mother—
dark sky, part moon, part mother:
exact same as light cream, sugar substitute.

Just 1/2 a moon, 1/2 a moon, 1/2 a moon onward.
Pointing, I said, I'll always say,
Look at the
Ring around the
and I cried a river then, the Pecos, the Puerco, the dream blue
    Navesink,
the banks of which I was born by.

Small, I drank my milky demitasse of coffee,
sweetened, matzoh crumbled in,

though I already
pointed at moons,

not through a café window,
the table's cloth crimson with the leakage of sweet fruit,
but through a child's eyes,
raised over a porcelain cup,
partway full.

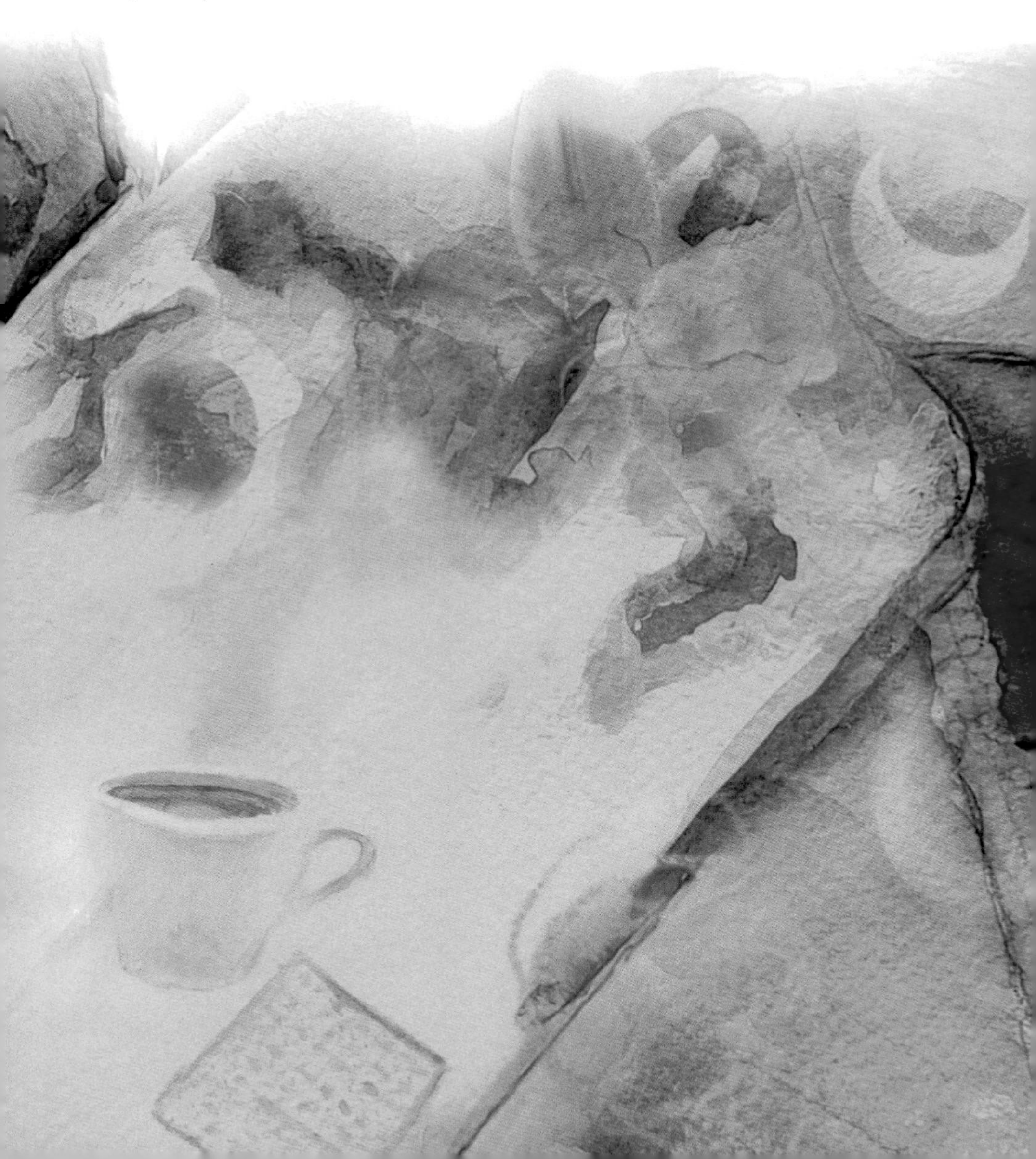

Entering the Dream Lodge

What sweetness to have sane family, she thought, watching her aunt settling the floppy hat more firmly on her head, painting the canyon's ridge glowing in the huge gold moon of September.

—The Prana Fish, *Alexia Fortunati*

First frost that morning, but light.
Tomatoes nipped, but the cosmos made it.
Survival of scarlet runners a celebration,
likewise the gladiolus and marigolds.

Whatever's left, a gift of color.
Ice crystals melting from the pickup's windshield,
and at the kitchen window—but that's another story—

When the bear came, we stopped washing the dishes.
When the bear came, we were gabbing and gobbling,
sharing stories and giant chocolate chip cookies,
a huge eclair filled with cream.

The dough was rich, vanilla and crisp walnuts, sweet butter,
but the truth was the bear at the window.
Part myth, but the realest one in the night.
An invitation, a summoning
into winter silence, cave of quiet,
the drowsy gathering of soft bodies
tumbled amongst themselves in familial sleep.

We were a sink, a window and 3 worlds away.

When the bear came, we shrieked and chattered,
ran upstairs and down
excited, wanting, terrified of wild,
utterly thrilled.

Longing in our domestic hearts,
for the honey of that contact.

We entered together: 3 women, maiden, matron and elder.
Moon Women, reweaving the tattered warp of family
into the fine cloth of relations.
Wove it from the brown fur of bear,
his eyes wide and burnished bronze
from his bear world looking.

When the bear came, we were stirred, we were blended.
Platter of pastries, green chile asimmer, a circle of talk.
It was cauldron, cook pot,
out of the frying pan and into desire.
Learning to disappear, to reflect, to shine.
Everything we enter the kitchen to enact, happened,
when the bear came.

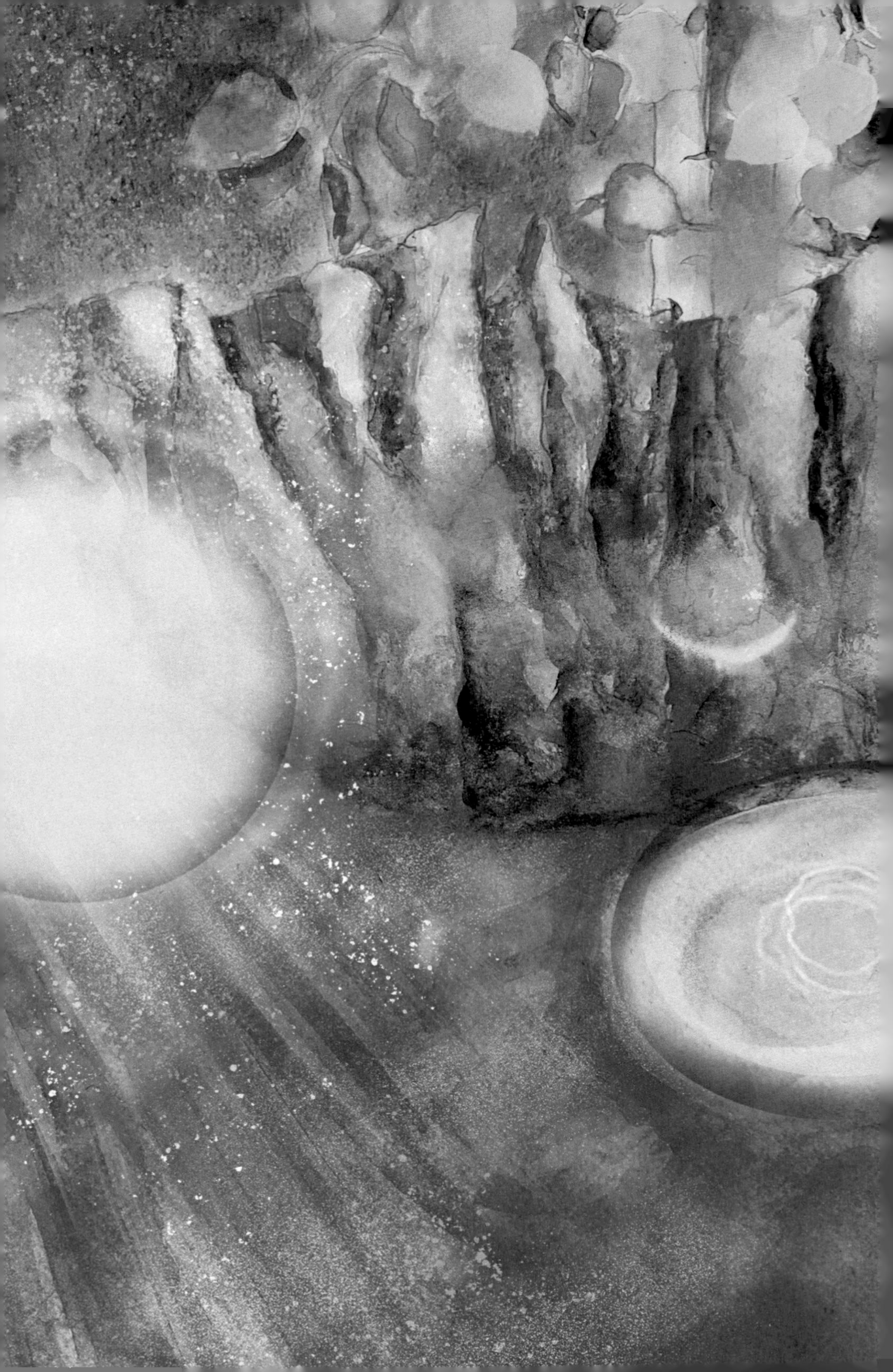

Slow Down and Meet the Fast Goddess

Slip between moon into solid fragrance.

Memorize the wisdom written on the face of glaciers.

Keep walking.
If this is the day the ground opens,
then it is.

Bake a cake of many grains and go down.
You will lose your mother—and gain a recipe.

Follow the rules:
Eat nothing
Don't linger

Love the fierce beauty of the taken daughter that is yourself.

Track mountain lion into the den of the invisible
become snake and vice
versa; curl & swirl, shimmer into Vendredi,
into Kali Durga, Pele, and La Diosa de Las Serpientes,
clamour of skulls around your waist.

Slip between seasons into the mythology of river.
Turn as aspens do, both under and gold.

Flicker into ripe.
Rhyme with sideways, with bangle, with breathless and the first
word for chaos you can think of —

the light right now is such a good guess.

Keep going.

Learn what is good enough to say twice.

Let's tangle with undying love—
take it on, take it on—
take on a round of immortal, burn all
the way to ash and rise as berry.

Hunter's Moon: come find me,
I'm in full décolleté camo,
dressed as cattail and raven's caw, braceleted in fallen grasses.

If you are first frost, let me be your early thaw.

We'll make a supple weather out of amnesia, inscribe
remembering on clouds.

I want to dive, cirrus, into your name,
nimble one, all clues aside,
I'll come up hooked.

Reel me in, back to this world,
from that,

I wriggle, good god, moon fish,
shining in your breathing hands.

Day of Two Snakes

Walked late,

past a curve of copper colored oak,
a stand of Virginia creeper ablaze.
Eyes on the horizon, I missed, almost,
the garter, run down mid-road.

Enticed by the warm dust,
slowed by the cooling air,
he's sunned his last on this earth.

I never see snakes, ex-lovers or ghosts.
It's just easier that way.

Today my terror caught me,
it was time.

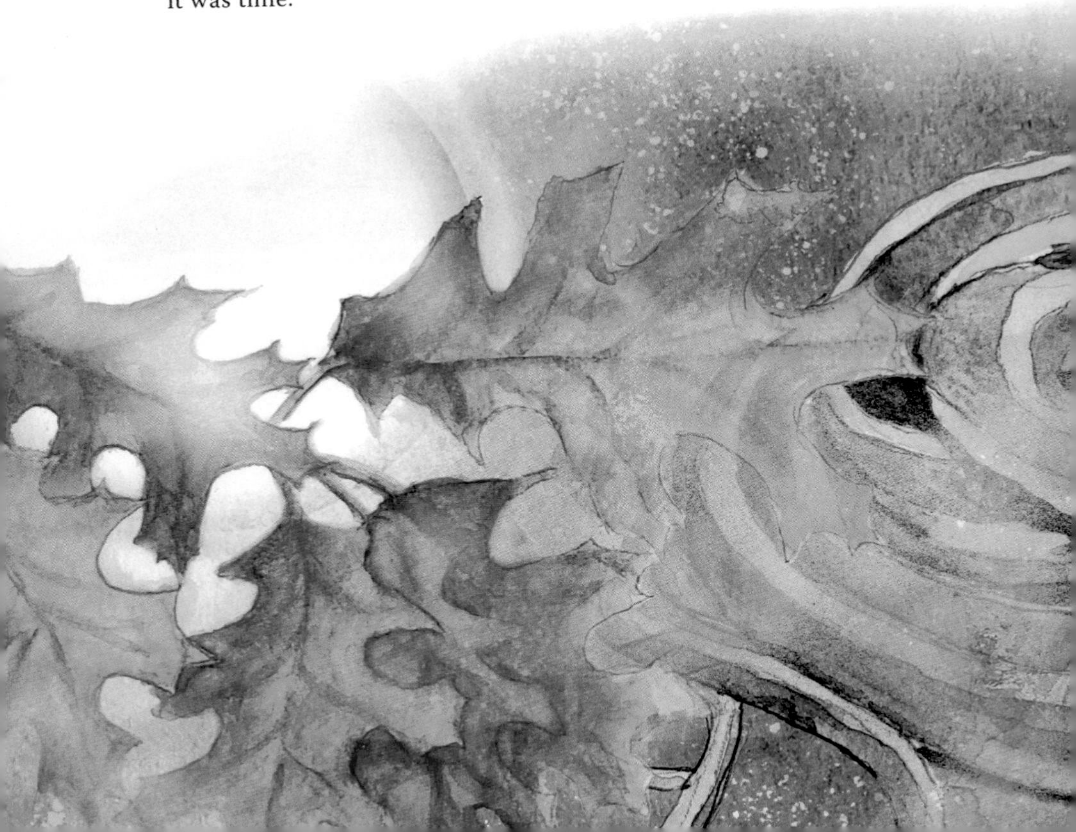

I've vowed to see snakes.

It was simple, as if coil and curve,
the slither and sleek, sudden appearance
of what we've loved or loathed
is a piece of a puzzle.

Or maybe just a turn in the road.
Just that.

By October's Blood Moon, the Hunter's Moon,
I seek no elk,
nor wait in blinds, poised for winged presence.

I stalk nothing, am myself stalked
by what I've missed,
in leaves turning, what I have turned from.

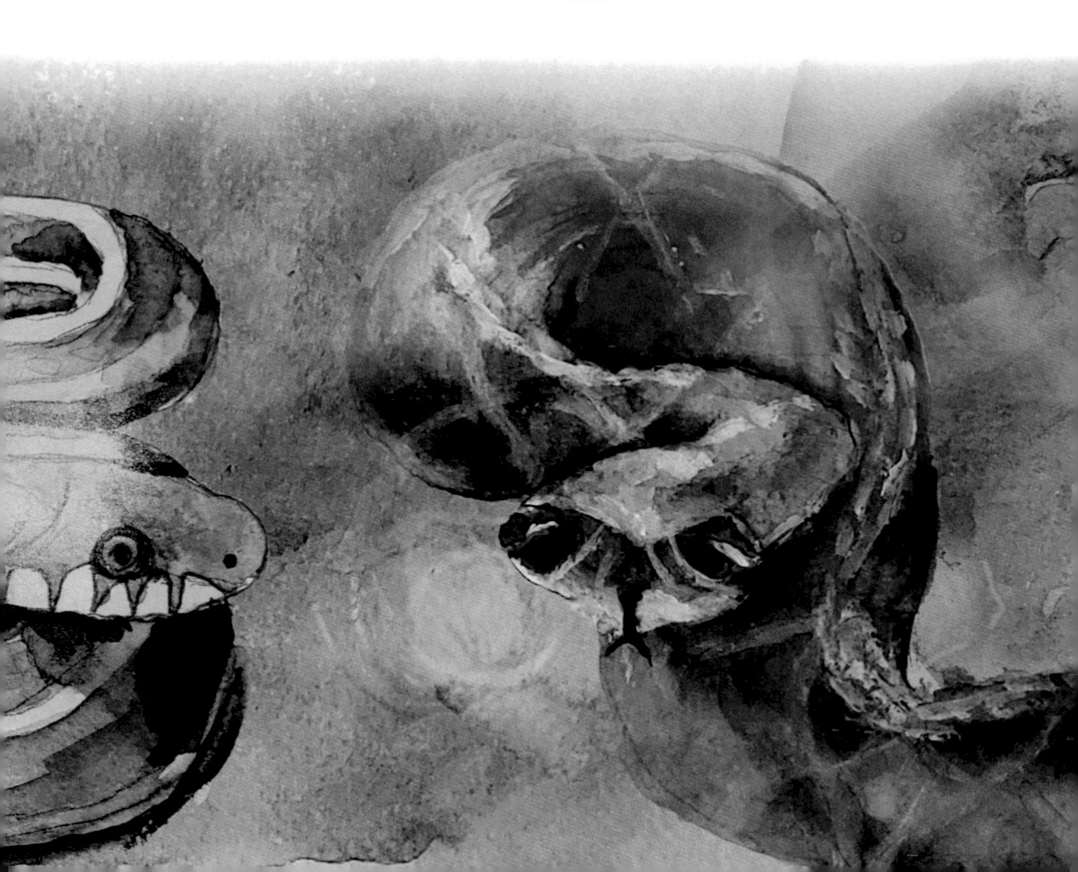

Moon This Season

Saw the Beaver Moon, but it wasn't madness.
Just that, full November,
Soft Snow.

Every Buck Loves His Antlers, Then Loses Them Moon.
Striped Gopher Looks Back Moon, the Assiniboine people say.
And they ought to know.

Last night in dream, Robert Bly kissed me,
or maybe just inhaled my perfume ecstatically
& I'm exaggerating,
pretending to know famous poets in my dreams.

He gave me and my sister a robot of spalted maple,
showing even good wood has a home in my nights.

It was 12H again, as ever,

and yes, Mom Appeared.
This dream starred Mom and a gorgeous ring
on the bejeweled hand of the beautiful black woman,
whom the robot awoke into when we found her key
and turned it.

She came with stacks and piles of printouts,
Gnostic wisdom, Kabbalah, theorems and equations.
She told me something so interesting,
what was it?

I can't predict what this may have to do with eternity.
Or rebirth.

I do know this about the Nativity, though:
everyone was there, that needed to be there.

Goslings, camels, grain and gold, the stable,
fragrant herbs, warm oils, a burro, or two,
starlight slipping through ceiling joists,

Bees, I am hoping, and their startling honey,
and the erotic questions posed by hum and buzz.

And me, I think, and you,
and the words we will need to say this
come morning.

Only the Holy

The bed is not made, and the bread is not kneaded
and the bells that ring in the temple of the woman alone
do not summon the quiet one,
whose broom does not sweep the leaves,
the leaves that do not fall.

After the snow did not fall, because snow had already fallen
and the echo of those bells rang out
into a room so filled with empty
that you'd have to invent bowls and bones
and nests and baskets to write this.

You must plant a peace rose.

Prune it over seven seasons, & save the thorns
from the cuttings. Write love spells on white candles.
Light those candles in empty rooms
that look out on snowy fields,
on scrub oaks, bare of leaves.

Then, then, then,
will the bells wild ring
will the bread rise,
and we, we, beloveds, will go to our shared bed,
to dream the moongarden that will grow that rose.

Acknowledgments

Enormous gratitude to my teacher and mentor, Dolores LaChapelle, who set me on the path of studying the Moon through time and across cultures...providing, as she always did, textual resources and wisdom from her voluminous files...and told all of us so privileged to be in her orbit: "Become the Bard of your place..."

Gratitude for all those mornings with Art Goodtimes on her front steps, and so...

Gratitude to poet Art Goodtimes—human dynamo and my Beloved—co-creator of Talking Gourds community and Mushroom Festival (and and and...!) who introduced so many of us to Dolores...and inspires us always and ever with his shimmering brilliance.

to my fellow MoonWriters over all the years at Rockmirth—Zoë Bird, Rachelle Woods, Jane Lipman, Dale Harris, et alia...thank you, dear friends, for your Moon Poems and being such juicy companions on this ride!

to Frances Woods, our phenomenal proofreader, for her exquisite attention to detail and sensitivity to the Voice of our writers... yours are the finishing touches of perfection; you make our books shine!

and to my partner at Wild Rising Press, Mary M Meade, enormously gifted artist and book and graphic designer, her boundless enthusiasm on our projects, her cut-to-the-chase clarity. And ooh...thank you, Mary, for how much fun we have—making beautiful books together!

The text of these poems is set in Warnock pro, a unique 20th century typeface commissioned to honor—and mirror—the visionary spirit of John Warnock, co-founder of Adobe, inventor of the PDF, and programs enabling small-scale printing for the first time. Harkening back to classic fonts, with modern notes, this is a timeless font whose origin is suffused with gratitude, with loving respect for invention, created to recognize the generosity inherent in the art and craft of all aspects of making books, and to give a Gift. These poems were written in exactly this spirit: to honor Her Light—Light that has lit our way, our nights, our imagination, measures our time, inspires poets and lovers, shifts our tides, inner and outer. The titles are set in Vendetta OT, also created as an homage. Based on a famous Venetian typeface developed in 1470 by iconic pioneer printer and type designer Nicolas Jensen, a pivotal force in the emergence of Venice as one of the first great centers of the printing press, Vendetta, with its lunaresque slopes, and full moon o's, was designed in the 1990s to revive and commemorate his seminal typefaces. These fonts marry old and new, and gift the poems with graceful clarity and tender, subtle legibility.

Made in the USA
Las Vegas, NV
11 November 2023